The Student
Survival Guide

The Student Survival Guide

By
Phil Chambers
&
Elaine Colliar

ECPC Publications
(A division of Learning Technologies Ltd)

Learning Technologies Ltd

Published by:
ECPC Publications
A division of Learning Technologies Ltd
The Forge
New Invention
Bucknell
Shropshire SY7 0BS
United Kingdom

www.mindmaptraining.com
www.learning-tech.co.uk

First Published 2004

A catalogue record for this book is available from the British Library

ISBN 1-904906-01-X

Cover design by Yves Van Damme (Pangraphics Ltd)

Prepress and typesetting by Pangraphics Ltd, Cupar, Scotland
Printed and bound by MMS Almac Ltd, Keith, Moray, Scotland

Dedication

This book is dedicated to every student who has ever thought that there must be an easier way to balance their studies, their hobbies and their lives. We hope that by showing them the path travelled by students before them, they can find an easier route.

To my baby boy, James Daniel, a learning laboratory in our daily life together. The boy who has spurred me on to braver and bigger things than I could ever have dreamed possible.

Finally, to Eddie Mara, a remarkable teacher who first introduced me to Mind Mapping and changed the course of my life forever.

Elaine Colliar

To the excellent teachers who helped me throughout my school days and to those who now attend my seminars, taking the techniques in this book into classrooms around the World.

Phil Chambers

ACKNOWLEDGEMENTS

Tony Buzan - For Originating Mind Mapping
Rod Dumbreck - For technical help
Anne Jones - For proof reading and support
Vanda North - For training us both in the art of radiance

Contents List

Contents Mind Map

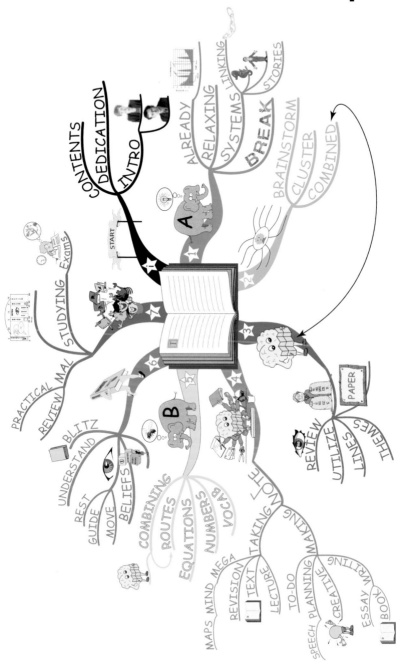

PHIL

Phil Chambers, a World Mind Mapping Champion, a five times Mind Sports Olympiad Medalist and International Master of Mind Mapping.

He has been a Buzan Licensed Instructor since 1995, trained by Tony Buzan (originator of Mind Mapping) and Vanda North (founder of Buzan Centres).

In addition to this, he is a certified Working Styles Analysis User, a Registered Accelerated Learning Trainer, a Practitioner of Neuro-Linguistic Programming (NLP), an Associate of the Chartered Institute of Personnel & Development (CIPD) and a member of the Professional Speakers Association.

Prior to entering the training profession, Phil worked as a computer programmer and has a BSc in Physics and Chemistry from the University of Durham. Drawing on this scientific background, he is one of the few people to successfully apply Mind Mapping to mathematics.

Phil is Chief Arbiter of the World Memory Sports Council and scorer of the Mind Sports Olympiad Memory and Speed Reading events. He is a founder member of the Mind Sports Council and his contribution to Mind Sports won him the "Special Services to Memory" award in 1996.

His Mind Maps have been published in Hodder & Stoughton's GCSE and A-Level Revision Guides, "The Learning Revolution", "Teaching Pupils How To Learn" and "A Mind to do Business".

You can contact Phil through his training company, Learning Technologies Ltd, at www.learning-tech.co.uk, which specialises in offering bespoke solutions enabling companies and individuals overcome problems and achieve their goals.

ELAINE

If ever there was a student that a teacher didn't want in their classroom, it was probably Elaine Colliar: Dyslexic, dyspraxic, unable to sit still - "A smart child, if only she would apply herself". Destined never to be an academic success. After discovering some of the skills you will find in this book, she went on to demonstrate academic brilliance and found a passion for lifelong learning.

Now Elaine Colliar is the five times World Mind Mapping Champion, reigning Mind Sports Olympiad Mind Mapping Champion and an International Grand Master of Mind Mapping. She hosts seminars in Mind Mapping, Memory, Mental and Financial Literacy around the world. Her passion is working with children with learning differences.

Starting her working life in the West End as a Stage Manager and Club Manager, she is now classed as a serial entrepreneur. Elaine has founded a string of companies including:

Btex Limited
Software and website development company, developers of the award winning www.streetmap.co.uk

Elaine Colliar Limited
A highly successful corporate training company
www.mindmaptraining.com

Building Success Ltd
A residential property investment company.

Invest n Share Ltd
A company that teaches groups and individuals to utilize Mind Maps to maximise the returns they can achieve through investing in the stock market.
www.investnshare.com

She is an arbiter for the Mind Sports Olympiad, including the Memory and Speed Reading events. She was also co-author of the "Single Mom's guide to..." series.

x

CHAPTER ONE

MEMORY PART A

MEMORY PART A

INTRODUCTION

WHAT YOU
ALREADY DO

RELAXATION
AND MEMORY

LINK SYSTEM

SEAHORSE
PRINCIPLES

BODY SYSTEM

YOUR REVIEW

BREAKS

SUMMARY

In this section we will explore what you already do to remember and forget and discover your brain's natural memory rhythms.

You will see how to:

Improve your memory with a simple link system and how this can be made stronger by using some general principles.

Use your body to help you remember!

Review information easily that has been memorised in a brain friendly way.

Boost recall by taking breaks.

To begin, give yourself 2 minutes to try to remember the following list of words...

book	the	and
of	and	stop
the	hand	own
white	walk	time
and	work	hold
of	William Shakespeare	of
end	candle	house
the	hill	coat

3

INTRODUCTION

**WHAT YOU
ALREADY DO**

RELAXATION
AND MEMORY

LINK SYSTEM

SEAHORSE
PRINCIPLES

BODY SYSTEM

YOUR REVIEW

BREAKS

SUMMARY

WHAT YOU
ALREADY DO

Can you recall all the words in the correct order?

1 _____	9 _____	17 _____
2 _____	10 _____	18 _____
3 _____	11 _____	19 _____
4 _____	12 _____	20 _____
5 _____	13 _____	21 _____
6 _____	14 _____	22 _____
7 _____	15 _____	23 _____
8 _____	16 _____	24 _____

If you can't answer this test correctly, don't worry. The list is designed to be too long for you to remember on reading it through once unless you are using a memory system.

Psychologists have determined that, on average, you can hold 7±2 pieces of data in short-term memory at the same time.

Can you remember any of the first few words?

Can you remember the exact middle word?

Can you recall any of the last words?

Did any words jump out at you as being unusual?

Did any of the words you read have any strong associations for you – or did any of the words you read combine to make a single mental picture or thought?

Did you recognise if any of the words were repeated?

On average the recall pattern looks like this...

So to make things more memorable you need to:

⭐ Have more beginnings and ends to your learning.

⭐ Repeat or link things together to create strong associations.

⭐ Make things unusual or outstanding.

RELAXATION
AND MEMORY

Has your mind ever gone blank in the middle of an exam?

Have you ever had someone's name 'on the tip of your tongue'?

You knew that you knew it but couldn't quite remember it and the harder you tried to remember the more elusive the memory became. Then when you stopped trying and relaxed the information just popped into your head.

What physically happens when you are stressed is that your brain goes into 'fight or flight' mode - Faced with danger the best survival strategy inherited from our caveman ancestors was to fight or run away. Blood and oxygen are diverted from the upper part of your brain where memories are stored down to your muscles. So you're physically strengthened but mentally weakened.

The way to stop your mind from going blank is to avoid getting stressed. There are some simple relaxation techniques which, when practiced regularly, will allow you to enter a state of relaxed alertness that is ideal for learning whenever you need to.

Here's what you do:

- Find somewhere quiet and comfortable to sit, away from distractions.
- Close your eyes and breath in through your nose and out through your mouth. With each out breath give a little sigh 'ahh' and count slowly backwards from ten to one. With each number feel the stress drain out of you.
- Imagine being somewhere tranquil where you can you feel relaxed and safe. Perhaps on a warm tropical beach, in a forest or in the mountains. Imagine the sights, smells, sounds, tastes and physical sensations as if you were really there.
- Spend as long as you like.
- When you're ready to return, count slowly back from one to ten, the scene fading with each number. When you reach ten, open your eyes and feel refreshed and relaxed.

THE LINK MEMORY SYSTEM

The Link System is one of the simplest memory systems but is none the less quite powerful. It makes use, primarily, of the fact that you remember associated items.

To remember a list you take each item and associate it in some way with the next. This forms a chain of associations that can easily be recalled.

If the list contains abstract concepts these will need to be symbolised by concrete objects.

As an example, let's try to memorise the first 10 chemical elements in the Periodic Table:

Hydrogen	Carbon
Helium	Nitrogen
Lithium	Oxygen
Beryllium	Fluorine
Boron	Neon

These can be remembered as follows...

Imagine a huge tower-block sized, shiny red fire hydrant (HYDROGEN). As you walk past you look up and see millions of helium - filled (HELIUM) balloons tied to the top of the hydrant. There are so many that they begin to lift the hydrant up off the ground and into the air.

As it rises into the evening sky, you follow its route, as it is lit by the intense white light (LITHIUM) shining from thousands of berries (BERYLLIUM) on a nearby tree. At the base of the tree is an ugly wart-faced smelly wild boar (BORON) digging at the roots and throwing up a pile of dirty black coal (CARBON).

The dust and soot from the ever increasing pile of coal blocks out the Sun and causes a false night (NITROGEN). The airborne dust makes it so hard for you to breathe that you don a diving suit and oxygen tank (OXYGEN). You struggle to waddle forward wearing your flippers, this makes you sweat and breathe heavily.

You remove your mask and you realise that you are coming down with a case of the flu (FLUORINE). You begin to cough and splutter and as you sneeze you spray mucus over a massive neon (NEON) sign in the shape of a number 10 that blinks on and off in front of you.

SEAHORSE PRINCIPLES

In simple terms, memories are pictures that you create in your head. The clearer and more detailed the picture – the easier it is to recall.

By using the following 8 easy principles to add to the pictures you create in your head you will be able to make unforgettable memories with ease:

Senses

Making a memory more "multi-sensory" by using as many of your senses as you can (ie sight, sound, smell, taste and touch) will make the memory trace much stronger and easier to recall.

Exaggeration

By creating pictures that are larger, louder, smellier, sweeter, sourer and more tactile you can boost what you remember.

Action

Create your images with as much action as possible. A full-colour horse galloping through a field with its rippling muscles, flowing mane and high pitched whinny is more memorable than a black and white image of a static horse.

Humour

Things that make you smile, giggle or groan – even bad jokes and puns will increase your enjoyment of learning and therefore increase your memory.

Order

Ordered items are easier to recall than those all jumbled up. One of the first ways we learn is when our carers tell us stories where things must happen in a certain order.

Repetition

Repetition – especially at the appropriate times boosts what you can remember. It reinforces the memory pathways in the brain making it easier and easier to remember what you are trying to learn every time you return and do a review of that information.

Symbols

Using symbols boosts recall – especially as memories are pictures. Substituting abstract or ordinary items with extraordinary symbols will make them easier to remember. (more about how you use symbolism to translate information into an easier to remember form later...)

Enjoy

Using your memory and your imagination to learn should be easy and fun. If you can make it fun to do, you will want to keep doing it – a well trained imagination will help make memorising a delight.

By combining the SEAHORSE principles with any of the memory or study systems you will greatly improve your ability to remember any information that you choose.

The hippocampus, a structure in the centre of the brain thought to be responsible for memory is so called because of its SEAHORSE-like shape.

THE BODY LIST SYSTEM

Have you ever written down a list of things you need to remember – and then discovered that you can't remember where you put the list?

Here is an easy technique that helps you create a useful short term memory system that will help you remember any things that you would normally put on a list - ie shopping lists, to-do lists, etc.

NOTE: If you don't use the other systems in this book then this is the technique you need for cramming if all else fails!

The body has a number of parts in set locations that can act as places (or hooks) to 'hang' objects in your imagination:

Head
Nose
Neck
Shoulders
Chest
Hands
Stomach
Hips
Knees
Feet

Remember to use
SEAHORSE

For example, to remember the first three items of a shopping list...

ON YOUR FEET:
Imagine you are balanced on a pile of eggs. You are too heavy for them and they smash, 'squishing' yolk between your toes as you smell their rotten stench.

BETWEEN YOUR KNEES:
A loaf of French bread - Smell the aroma of a fresh 2m long loaf that you have to walk in an awkward way to stop from falling.

ON YOUR HIPS:
A bunch of bananas on each hip: Huge, dangling, fluorescent yellow.

YOUR REVIEW

To show just how easy it is to memorise information using these techniques and to act as a review, try to fill in the blanks for the examples that we have used so far in this section...

What do the letters in **SEAHORSE** stand for?

S_____

E_____

A_____

H_____

O_____

R_____

S_____

E_____

What were the three shopping list items?

_____

_____

_____

Fill in the blanks in the Periodic Table story:

Imagine a huge tower-block sized, shiny red fire hydrant (_____). As you walk past you look up and see millions of _____ - filled (_____) balloons tied to the top of the hydrant. There are so many that they begin to lift the hydrant up off the ground and into the air.

As it rises into the evening sky, you follow its route, as it is lit by the intense white light (_____) shining from thousands of _____ (BERYLLIUM) on a nearby tree. At the base of the tree is an ugly wart-faced smelly wild boar (_____) digging at the roots and throwing up a pile of dirty black coal (_____).

The dust and soot from the ever increasing pile of coal blocks out the Sun and causes a false night (_____). The airborne dust makes it so hard for you to breathe that you don a diving suit and _____ tank (_____). You struggle to waddle forward wearing your flippers, this makes you sweat and breathe heavily.

You remove your mask and you realise that you are coming down with a case of the __ (FLUORINE). You begin to cough and splutter and as you sneeze you spray mucus over a massive _____ (_____) sign in the shape of a number 10 that blinks on and off in front of you.

If you made any mistakes, try to analyse why. Was it because you didn't imagine the picture vividly enough? Perhaps our associations weren't strong enough? -Your own associations will always be best for you.

INTRODUCTION

WHAT YOU
ALREADY DO

RELAXATION
AND MEMORY

LINK SYSTEM

SEAHORSE
PRINCIPLES

BODY SYSTEM

YOUR REVIEW

☞ BREAKS

SUMMARY

16

BREAKS

MYTH

In order to learn something you have to hit the books for hours and hours until you have drilled it into your head.

TRUTH

The best way to learn is to approach it as 'little and often'. Work for a while, then when your brain starts to daydream, or wander, or drift away, or get bored, *STOP*, take a break and start learning again.

You can actually remember much more from a period of learning if you break it down into little chunks than if you do it all in one go...

So you can recall more by working less. Don't work harder, **work smarter**!

SUMMARY

When studying:

⭐ Have more beginnings and ends to your learning.

⭐ Repeat or link things together to create strong associations.

⭐ Make things unusual or outstanding.

Practice relaxation techniques to avoid stress in exams.

The Link System can be used to remember simple lists.

The Sea Horse Principles aid and reinforce memory systems:

Senses
Exaggeration
Action
Humour
Order
Repetition
Symbols
Enjoy

The Body List system can be used to remember 10 items or more.

Take regular breaks whilst studying to boost recall.

CHAPTER TWO

BRAINSTORMING & CLUSTERING

BRAINSTORMING

CLUSTERING

COMBINING THE
TECHNIQUES

Brainstorming is a way to express and freely associate ideas as they come to you without the need to classify them. Write down everything that comes to mind without judging the ideas. A 'stupid' idea can often lead to a 'good' idea that you may not have otherwise thought of.

Begin by drawing a picture of the topic that you're thinking about in the centre of your sheet of paper with lines radiating outwards.

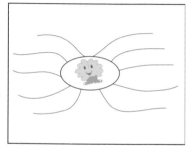

Write words or draw pictures of the ideas on these lines. If you run out of ideas add extra lines, as the brain likes to complete things and will generate enough ideas to fill the available spaces.

If you find that an idea that you have written triggers related ideas, these can be written on smaller lines off the main ones....

You can even add
lines to the lines...

and so on....

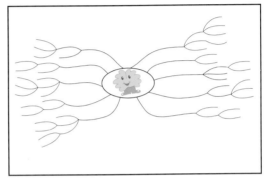

For ever ...
and ever...
and ever...

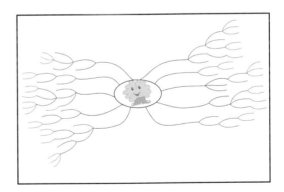

CLUSTERING

Once you have taken your thinking wide with a
brainstorm, it is often useful to improve the focus and
clarity of your ideas by grouping them together into
categories...

For example if your brainstorm generated the following ideas...

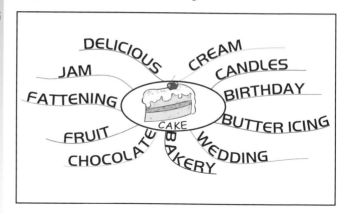

These could be grouped into:

Ingredients
Occasions
Feelings
Places

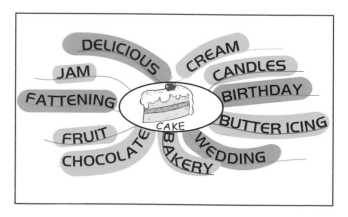

These categories can be used as the main branches of a Mind Map - The technique that we'll show you in the next section of this book...

COMBINING THE TECHNIQUES

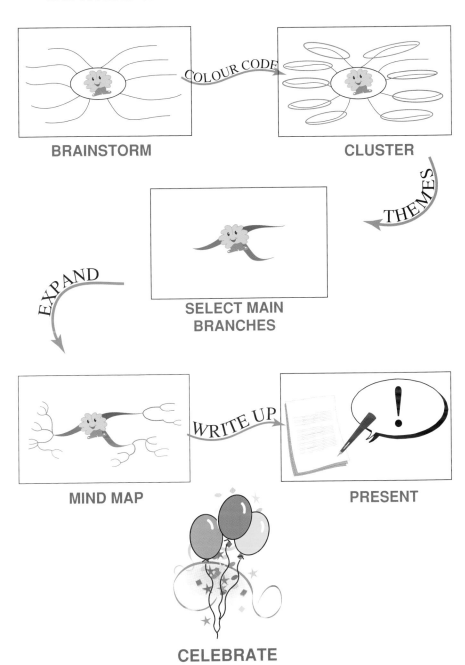

BRAINSTORM

COLOUR CODE

CLUSTER

THEMES

SELECT MAIN
BRANCHES

EXPAND

MIND MAP

WRITE UP

PRESENT

CELEBRATE

CHAPTER THREE

MIND MAPPING RULES

INTRODUCTION

What is Mind Mapping?

Mind Mapping is the most efficient note making and note taking technique that we know.

It works in harmony with the rhythms of the brain by using images, associations, space and colour to encourage thought processes to flow and increase recall.

A Mind Map is a powerful graphical representation of your thoughts and ideas - reflecting on paper the structure of your brain and how it processes information.

In this section you will learn the rules that you follow to create a Mind Map. These are all based on psychological research and many years of experience and so you should try to adhere to them wherever possible, especially if you're using a Mind Map for studying or to increase your memory.

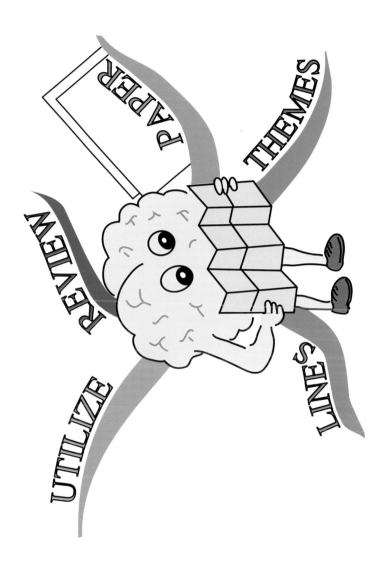

PAPER

THEMES

REVIEW

LINES

UTILIZE

THE RULES OF MIND MAPPING

Central Image

Create a unique and therefore memorable central image for each Mind Map you make. If you feel your artwork lets you down, get creative and copy, cut and paste, photocopy or print out a central image from another source.

Take the time to make a beautiful starting point to your Mind Map - using at least 3 colours will boost your recall by making the unique image more memorable, but use as many colours as you can.

By taking the time and effort to make a central image you are preparing the brain to look forward to a learning experience.

PAPER

Use your paper landscape - because our writing tends to be longer than higher, this leaves you more room for branching out with your associations.

Use blank paper - if you use lined or squared paper you may find you use the straight lines for writing on rather than flowing outwards in a radiant way.

Use as large a piece of paper as you can - A3 paper will leave you plenty of space to capture lots of detail on your Mind Map. For ease of filing and to be able to carry the Mind Maps around school or college, why not fold and file them like this...

File by subject

Punch

Fold with a margin

A3 paper

LANDSCAPE
BLANK
LARGE
PAPER

central image with the less important details out towards the edges. The order flows from the 2 o'clock position clockwise.

WORDS

Mind Maps only use key words. They tend to be nouns and will usually comprise 5 – 10% of the words. This means that you will be capturing far fewer words taking notes on a Mind Map than if you were taking "traditional" linear notes. Printing words (in upper or lower case) helps the brain to "photograph" the words more easily to recall at a later date. Using one word per line allows you to make more associations from each word and so improve your memory.

THEMES - IMAGES

Start by creating a unique image in the centre of your paper. After reviewing you will discover that you can recreate the Mind Map in your mind's eye. A unique image will help you to do this. Use at least three colours to make the image more attractive and hence memorable. Don't draw a box around your central image. Leaving the image open with no boundaries drawn around it helps you to associate more freely and widely.

HIERARCHY

A Mind Map has a radiant hierarchy. The most important facts are clustered in close to the

Try to use no more than 7 main branches on each Mind Map (short term memory can hold 7±2 bits of information at a time) -fewer branches often lead to enhanced memory.

Using organic or wavy main branches in a Mind Map helps to draw the eye outwards. By using curved lines you are also best able to use the space on the paper, by curving the lines into the space available.

Using one colour for each branch provides an extra memory hook to increase the ease with which you can recall your information - "It's on the green branch"... "It's a long word, etc."

LINES

Make the length of each line equal to the length of the keyword or image on it. Too short and it won't fit, too long and you waste space! Make sure that each line connects to the end of the previous line and that the lines radiate out from the centre. Often if you leave a gap between lines you will fail to recall things 'downstream' of the break.

The lines should decrease in size and hence importance towards the outside of the Mind Map. At the centre they are thick like the branches of a tree, becoming thinner and thinner before tapering off into tiny twigs.

35

UTILIZE

Mind Mapping is a fun and creative way of making and taking notes. To keep the fun, keep your brain engaged and to help boost your recall, try to improve each Mind Map by increasing the use of each of these concepts every time.

If information is very important or relevant, you can use perspective to make the image look 3-dimensional rather than making it look flat – the information will then jump off the Mind Map and into your memory.

Make each new Mind Map just a little bit more beautiful to your own senses. Use lettering that you enjoy looking at, your favourite colours and images.

Have fun creating your Mind Map – if something is fun to do then you want to do more of it. So include humour, jokes, cartoons, puns (especially terrible ones)!

A Briefcase!

We are programmed to enjoy colour. All around us in the natural world there is vibrant colour. Rather than create boring, monotonous, monotone notes in black pen on white paper, rejoice in using multi-coloured pens, pencils, paints etc on the best quality paper you can find. Have fun experimenting with the hundreds of makes of pens on the market; fat pens; thin nibs; gel colours, glitter pens and scented pens. Use as many different types as you can to boost what you can remember.

ARROWS

One of the best ways to increase your understanding of the world – and to improve your exam grades at the same time is to become aware of how information is connected together.

The difference between an 'A' grade and an 'A plus' is the ability to show how knowledge from one subject connects to another.

You should not be surprised if the same word crops up on more than one branch of your Mind Map. This shows that the repeated word is a new theme running through the topic that you may not have seen had you been using linear notes. When you notice a word appearing on multiple branches you can reinforce the connection and hence your memory of the information by linking each occurrence with arrows.

Leonardo da Vinci said, "Study the Art of Science and the Science of Art. Develop the senses and realise that everything is connected to everything else".

As well as being used as a shorthand for particular concepts, codes can be used to indicate connections between related ideas. For example, if the same word occurs several times in a Mind Map you could either link each occurrence with an arrow or simply put the same code symbol (such as a star) next to each occurrence.

You can also colour code your Mind Map - For example on a 'things to do' Mind Map you can use highlighter pens to code urgent things in pink, things that rely on other people in blue and completed things in yellow. Similarly on a revision Mind Map important or related concepts can be colour coded in the same way.

SENSES

Have you ever smelt a certain scent like the smell of fresh bread or a particular brand of perfume and been vividly reminded of a distant memory. It's not just smells that evoke powerful memories. Every experience is a combination of inputs from all your senses - So try to use words and images on your Mind Maps that evoke as many of your other senses as possible.

CODES

Letters and words are just codes that symbolise ideas - Likewise, road signs, icons on your computer, musical notes and numbers are also codes. Try to build up a library of your own code symbols that represent concepts that occur regularly on your Mind Maps.

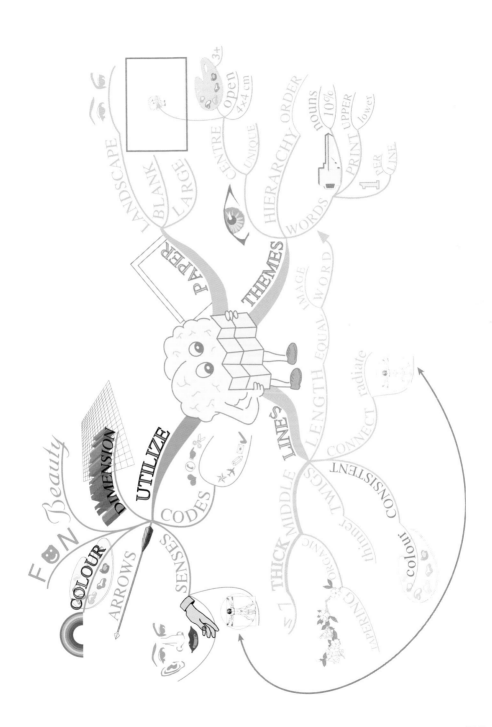

39

REVIEW

Be like the elephant – decide that you are never going to forget. By reviewing your Mind Maps at the appropriate times i.e. 10 minutes after creating, then 1 day, 1 week, 1 month and 3 months later you maximise your chances of remembering everything you have noted down.

To help you keep track of when you need to review, date the Mind Map at the bottom and enter the review codes:

10, D, W, M, 3M

Simply strike through the appropriate code after you have completed each review.

The beauty of reviewing using a Mind Map is that it can take so little time to do. A complex Mind Map containing a whole afternoon's learning can be reviewed in as little as 90 seconds. The entire review process takes less than 10 minutes to give you almost perfect recall of the information you have captured.

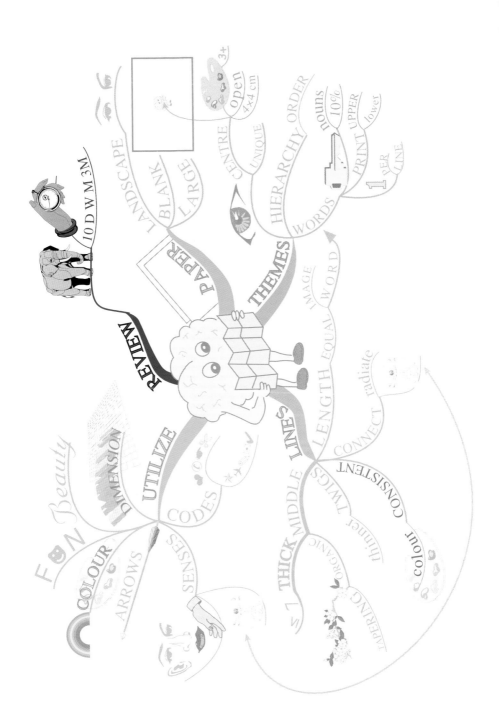

SUMMARY

CHAPTER FOUR

APPLICATIONS OF MIND MAPPING

INTRODUCTION

Having learned how to Mind Map we will now explore some of the many applications of Mind Maps in studying and everyday life.

Our list is neither meant to be prescriptive nor exhaustive. Once you begun to build confidence and become comfortable with the technique you will discover many more applications for Mind Maps.

The Applications can broadly be divided into two categories:

Note Making - Expressing your own ideas on paper.

WRITING A BOOK
AN ESSAY PLAN
A CREATIVE MIND MAP
PLANNING A SPEECH
TO-DO LIST

Note Taking - Taking someone else's ideas and understanding or remembering them.

LECTURE NOTES
NOTES FROM A TEXT BOOK
CURRICULUM REVISION
MEGA MIND MAPS

WRITING A BOOK

Using a Mind Map to plan the structure and content of a book before actually writing the text has a number of advantages.

* You know what you've covered and what you have still got to cover.

* You can write bits out of sequence – Without losing the overall flow of the entire book.

* It gives many people the ability to work on different bits of the book simultaneously.

* You can create the "easier" bits first before going on to the more "difficult" bits.

* You can create the book as a whole as opposed to a series of bits.

The majority of this book was written in two weeks using the Mind Map on the next page as a guide.

47

AN ESSAY PLAN

The Mind Map shows the inherent logic – ideal as an essay planner.

- Begin writing at 2 o'clock and work around the Mind Map step by step.

- Main themes, followed by argument, followed by evidence – footnotes. Repeat through each branch.

- Easy to give an overview, review and summary conclusions of your essay.

- Nothing goes adrift because of the logical progression of ideas.

- Your own associations shown by arrows on the Mind Map are those which earn you additional marks in essays – showing that you have understood the information and can connect it to other info that you have learned in other subject areas.

From an original Mind Map® by Anne Jones preparing to write an essay answering the question: "What do you think about presentation of the black characters in 'To Kill a Mockingbird'?"

CREATIVE MIND MAPS

Creativity is largely to do with making new and novel connections and associations. Since a Mind Map is a network of connections it is naturally suited to stimulate and support creative thoughts.

Creative Mind Maps differ from Study Mind Maps in several ways:

You do not have to restrict yourself to 7±2 branches. You are not aiming to remember the information on the Mind Map in the first instance. Merely to capture thoughts. You can produce a second refined Mind Map later.

Suspend judgment - To be truly creative you must be prepared to break outside the conventional. One way of doing this is to record absurd or 'stupid' thoughts that may lead to a new perspective.

Use as many pictures as possible - These can stimulate ideas more widely than words.

If you find yourself running out of ideas add an extra branch with nothing on it. The brain likes completion and will generate additional ideas to fill empty branches.

61

PLANNING A SPEECH

Mind Maps are a great way of organising your thoughts when planning a speech or presentation.

Try the following process:

Brainstorm what you already know about the topic. (see chapter 2)

Decide what content you want to include, discard irrelevant points.

Cluster the remaining information into between 5 and 9 categories. (These form the main branches of your Mind Map)

Decide on the order of the points and build up each branch in turn starting at the 'two o'clock' position and working around clockwise.

Research the subject, adding relevant data to the appropriate branch.

Review the Mind Map at the correct intervals. (see Chapter 3)

When you give the speech you only need the single page Mind Map with its key words to prompt you.

You may find that you can remember most of the content without referring to the Mind Map!

This is a Mind Map planning a whole day seminar that Elaine gave to a group of teachers and learning support staff. You should be able to recognise a lot of the content as it is similar to what we explain in this book.

A TO-DO 'LIST'

Mind Maps can be very useful for managing your time on a daily, weekly or monthly basis.

Because the structure of a Mind Map lets you summarise everything on a single page, you can immediately see connections and relationships that you might not otherwise have realised. For example, if something you need to do relies on getting information from someone else this can be indicated by an arrow or code.

Another advantage of using Mind Maps as to-do lists is that they are more memorable. Even without frequent review you are more likely to remember a colourful, image rich Mind Map than a single colour, linear list.

Once you have completed a task shown on your Mind Map, use a highlighter pen to strike off the relevant branch. This gives a good visual indication of what's done and what's still to do.

In the example on the next page we divided a circle into 24 sectors to represent 24 hours of a day. Then we colour coded them according to the planned activity that is described on the corresponding branches.

LECTURE NOTES

This is one of the most difficult Mind Maps to create as you tend to be doing it in "live time".

Try practicing on something not involved in your studies until you are confident of your ability to keep up – We suggest you try Mind Mapping parts of the TV news or something similar.

You are only trying to capture between 5 & 10% of the presented words. At the end of the lecture this will be even less – as your lecturer summarises, repeats or reviews the information covered.

To make it easier to Mind Map lectures on a regular basis – create a habit where you ask the lecturer in advance for the main topic and themes to be covered. You can then be one jump ahead by creating a unique central image and main branches before you even go into the lecture. This will leave you plenty of time to spend creating a beautifully creative and memorable Mind Map.

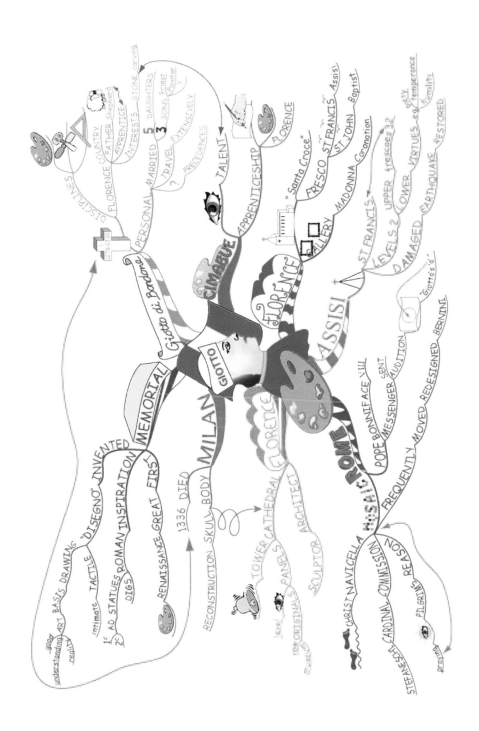

GIOTTO

DISCIPLINES

PERSONAL
- FLORENCE COUNTRY
- FATHER Shepherd
- APPRENTICE
- INTERESTS STONE carving
- MARRIED 5 DAUGHTERS
- 3 SONS Priest Painter
- ? TRAVEL EXTENSIVELY
- ? PRECEDENCES

Giotto di Bondone

TALENT
- APPRENTICESHIP
- FLORENCE

CIMABUE
- "Santa Croce" FLORENCE
- FRESCO ST FRANCIS Assisi
- ST JOHN Baptist
- MADONNA Coronation
- GALLERY

FLORENCE

ASSISI
- ST FRANCIS
- LEVELS 2 UPPER 4 frescoes 32
- LOWER VIRTUES e.g. Poverty Temperance Humility
- DAMAGED EARTHQUAKE RESTORED

ROME
- POPE BONNIFACE VIII
- MESSENGER SENT
- AUDITION "Giotto's o"
- FREQUENTLY MOVED REDESIGNED BERNINI
- MOSAIC
- STEFANESCHI CARDINAL COMMISSION
- NAVICELLA
- CHRIST
- REASON PILGRIMS praying

MILAN

FLORENCE
- TOWER CATHEDRAL
- ARCHITECT
- SCULPTOR PANELS level 100 ORIGINALS

1336 DIED
- RECONSTRUCTION SKULL BODY

MEMORIAL

"DISEGNO" INVENTED
- INSPIRATION
- RENAISSANCE GREAT FIRST
- ROMAN
- 1° AD STATUES DIGS
- 2°
- ART BASIS DRAWING
- Intimate TACTILE
- good understanding reality

NOTES FROM A TEXT BOOK (KEYWORDS)

Finding the keywords from a piece of written or spoken text is often thought to be the most difficult skill to acquire in Mind Mapping.

Keywords tend to be nouns and may only make up between 5 & 10% of the text being presented. They are easily identified as being the most important words or themes within that text.

You can make the words easy to find by highlighting them in your book or notes before you begin to Mind Map.

Within this explanation we have identified the keywords for you and represented in the portion of a Mind Map below…

KEYWORDS Thought difficult Themes nouns 5-10% Easy highlight notes Identified Mind Map

The example on the next page is a Mind Map of a whole chapter from a textbook.

Light & Sound

CURRICULUM REVISION

Using Mind Mapping as a revision aid has two main advantages...

- You can see an overview of the whole curriculum – This puts everything into its logical place.

- Mind Maps can be used for review – You can highlight branches as you finish your 5 times review.

Practice redrawing the Mind Map from memory. When you can do this you will never again be stumped for an answer in an exam – Simply redraw the Mind Map and begin your answer.

Review with friends by photocopying your Mind Map in black and white. "Read" the Mind Map to them to help them understand your associations. If they "colour in" the Mind Map as you share it and add their own images, codes and associations it will make the Mind Map personal and easier to remember.

Even better: Divide your curriculum by 5 and recruit 4 friends to produce a Mind Map of their section. You can all cover the entire curriculum in 20% of the time. The most difficult thing will be figuring out what to do with all your free time.

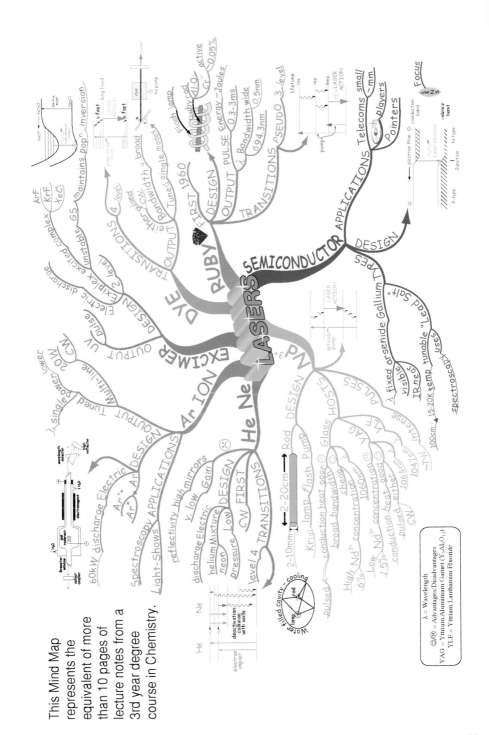

This Mind Map represents the equivalent of more than 10 pages of lecture notes from a 3rd year degree course in Chemistry.

MEGA MIND MAPS

Imagine you have an map of the World - It has countries and major cities labelled.

If you now look at a map or Britain - You see more detail - Motorways, towns, cities, main railway lines and major rivers.

Now take a road atlas - You see all the roads, villages, places of interest, etc.

Mind Maps are just the same. Notes from lectures or books are like the road atlas maps, containing lots of important detail but not easily placed in context. Curriculum revision Mind Maps may be a little less detailed and sum up the contents of a whole lecture on just one branch.

A Mega Mind Map is your map of the World. It covers an entire year's study on a single sheet of paper (At least A2 size, up to A0). Pin your Mega Mind Map to your wall and review it regularly. It won't contain all the detail of the course but will help you to identify the themes that run through it. By seeing, literally, the big picture you can make the connections that distinguish a B$^+$ student form an A or A$^+$.

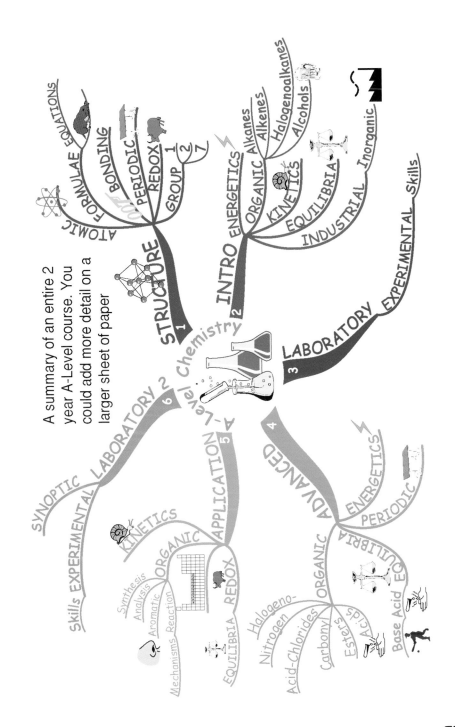

A summary of an entire 2 year A-Level course. You could add more detail on a larger sheet of paper

A-Level Chemistry

1 STRUCTURE
- ATOMIC
- FORMULAE EQUATIONS
- BONDING
- PERIODIC
- REDOX
- GROUP 1 / 2 / 7

2 INTRO
- ENERGETICS
- ORGANIC
  - Alkanes
  - Alkenes
  - Halogenoalkanes
  - Alcohols
- KINETICS
- EQUILIBRIA
- INDUSTRIAL Inorganic

3 LABORATORY
- EXPERIMENTAL Skills

4 ADVANCED
- ENERGETICS
- PERIODIC
- EQUILIBRIA
  - Acid Base
- ORGANIC
  - Halogeno-Nitrogen
  - Acid-Chlorides
  - Carbonyl
  - Esters
  - Acids

5 APPLICATION
- KINETICS
- ORGANIC
  - Synthesis
  - Analysis
  - Aromatic
  - Mechanisms Reaction
- REDOX
- EQUILIBRIA

6 SYNOPTIC LABORATORY 2
- Skills EXPERIMENTAL

63

CHAPTER
FIVE

MEMORY PART B

INTRODUCTION

You should by now be comfortable using some of the simpler memory systems such as the **Body List**, the **Link System** and using your ability to create strong memories by creating images using the SEAHORSE principles…

We will now show you some of the systems that the World's greatest Memory Champions use. These are not systems that are similar to the ones they use, but **exactly** the same – They just use them for recalling much larger chunks of information than you will need at the moment. To pass exams you need to be able to run for a bus – World Champions in the memory field need to be able to run Marathons in record breaking times. Don't get disheartened if you feel you still have a huge way to go to get to where the champions are – By using the systems in this book you will still be better informed and studying more efficiently than the majority of students around the planet.

The route system that we will learn about in this section is a more advanced version of the **Body List**, but instead of memorising ten bits of information, what you can memorise is limited only by your imagination.

FOREIGN VOCABULARY

Learning foreign language vocabulary is often a challenge for students struggling to associate the new word to something they already know.

To make this process easier, try linking each English word with its French equivalent by creating imaginary pictures or situations. If you apply the SEAHORSE principles and take care to use a situation or picture in which the link word closely matches the correct French pronunciation you will find your recall is greatly enhanced.

The more fun you have creating memorable imaginary pictures the easier they will be to recall, but you can also increase your recall by capturing your images in Mind Map form and following the suggested review process of 10 minutes, 1 day, 1 week, 1 month and three months. A large vocabulary in your Long term Memory will make it easier to locate the correct word when you are writing or speaking the new language.

For Example:

1. The French for **BREAD** is PAIN
   (pronounced PAHN)

Imagine that you are cramming
hundreds of French bread sticks into
a pan and are jumping up and down
on top of the lid to try and get it to fit.

2. The French for **WINE** is VIN
   (pronounced VAHN)

Imagine standing in a street feeling
very, very thirsty. You yank open the
rear door of a massive white van
and thousands of bottles of wine
cascade from the back, shattering
on the road and swamping you in a
pool of fruity smelling wine.

3. The French for **MENU** is CARTE
   (pronounced KART)

You are trying to order in a
restaurant – your waiters are riding
around in little go–carts and every
time they whiz past your table you
make a frantic effort to try and reach
out and grab a menu from one of
them.

INTRODUCTION

FOREIGN
VOCABULARY

☞ NUMBERS

EQUATIONS

THE ROUTE
SYSTEM

COMBINING
ROUTES AND
MIND MAPS

NUMBERS

Numbers are abstract concepts. They are hard to memorise because memories are pictures and abstract concepts are not.

To make memorising simpler all you have to do is represent the number as a picture of an object. One way to do this is to use the following code where each number is represented by a letter contained within a phonetic alphabet.

"In order for you to learn the method, you must first learn a simple phonetic alphabet…. With a different consonant sound for each of the digits. I'll make this simple for you by giving you a 'memory aid' for remembering each one"

Harry Lorayne
Memory Pioneer

No. Sound Memory aid

0 s or z first sound of the word "zero"
1 d or t both have only one downstroke
2 n   written n has two downstrokes
3 m   written m has three downstrokes
4 r   last sound of the word "four"
5 l   Roman numeral for 50 is "L"
6 g   letter g turned around looks like 6
7 k   two 7's together form a K
8 f   handwritten f ($\mathcal{f}$) looks like an 8
9 b or p the number 9 turned around is like b or p

Take pairs of digits from the number you wish to remember and substitute with letters using the table above. You can create words by adding vowels, which you then string together using a link system, as you did earlier with the periodic table.

Eg. To remember the number pi: $\pi \approx$ **3.14159**

3.1 = m t = mat

41 = r t = rat

59 = l b = lab

Imagine a welcome mat placed outside your chemistry classroom where a giant rat, demonstrating a practical lab experiment, throws a custard pie in your face.

EQUATIONS

INTRODUCTION

FOREIGN
VOCABULARY

NUMBERS

☞ EQUATIONS

THE ROUTE
SYSTEM

COMBINING
ROUTES AND
MIND MAPS

We use a similar method to make equations more memorable by turning them into pictures.

These pictures can again be remembered by using the link system and the SEAHORSE principles or combined with the route technique that we will look at next...

For example, a particularly useful but hard to remember equation (if you're not using a technique) is the formula for solving quadratic equations.

Where: $ax^2 + bx + c = 0$

$$x = \frac{-b \pm \sqrt{b^2 - 4ac}}{2a}$$

We can associate each symbol in turn with a picture related to it by either the same sound or a rhyme

Remember to use
S
E
A
H
O
R
S
E

x   x-ray

=   eagle

-       Midas (gold)

b   bee

and so on...

So the beginning of the 'link' story reads:

"Imagine you're x-raying an eagle. Inside his chest is a pot of gold but covered in honey being collected by thousands of bees."

THE ROUTE SYSTEM

INTRODUCTION

FOREIGN
VOCABULARY

NUMBERS

EQUATIONS

☞ **THE ROUTE
SYSTEM**

COMBINING
ROUTES AND
MIND MAPS

This is one of the oldest recorded memory systems, used by the Ancient Greeks and Romans, but as our brains have not significantly changed in what they are capable of in the last 2500 years, what they did then is still as applicable today.

Routes work on the same basis as the **Body List** – You create an image of the information you wish to remember and link it, instead of to a location on your body, onto a place along a very familiar journey or route.

Think of a route or journey that you know well and can travel along in your imagination. As you take the journey there will be a series of places or landmarks that you pass along the way. These will always be the same whenever you take the journey and will always be passed in the same order. These 'loci' are used as hooks to 'hang' the information to be remembered on.

For example your landmarks could be:

Front door   Gate   Post box   Traffic lights   Iron fence   Bench   Play area

Whilst you can easily use outside routes to hang your information on, the method I used to study for five A-Levels was to use a different room in my house for each subject. I used my bedroom for Biology, the living-room for English and the hall for Art History.

Here's an example of one of the routes I used:

There are lots of locations around the room, these can be as small as the light switch or as large as the wardrobe.

I imagined an object symbolising a different aspect of biology in each place: jeans for genetics, a plant for photosynthesis, a plate of sandwiches for digestion, etc.

Remember to use
SEAHORSE

INTRODUCTION

FOREIGN
VOCABULARY

NUMBERS

EQUATIONS

☞ THE ROUTE
SYSTEM

COMBINING
ROUTES AND
MIND MAPS

THE ROUTE SYSTEM
SUMMARY

- Prepare in your mind a well known route.

- Select locations along your route in the order you come across them.

- Using the SEAHORSE principles, create an image of the information you need to remember.

- Attach the image to each location in order along your route.

- Review your route thoroughly. You'll soon find that you are able to remember your information forwards and backwards, by traveling both ways along your route.

You can also learn to combine the Route techniques with other systems such as Mind Mapping. You can either place Mind Maps along your routes, or routes onto your Mind Maps.

ROUTES ON MIND MAPS

You create your Mind Map as usual adding the various aspects of theory on the branches. You then add another branch on which you draw the first location along your route where you have recorded data related to the theory (e.g. in our example the front door is the first location used to store the formula for solving quadratic equations)

When you come to review your Mind Map you will see the picture of the front door and run through the route In your imagination before moving on to the next branch.

MIND MAPS AND ROUTES

When Mind Mapping, you are encouraged to create a unique 'Central Image' to help you remember the Mind Map after your 5-times review. By setting up a route to use for each subject, I was able to associate the central image to a place on my route. Recalling the location with the central image from the Mind Map placed in it would then allow me to easily recreate the whole Mind Map in my imagination.

The central image of a pair of faded denim jeans (Genetics) was associated to my wardrobe. In my imagination, I could open the door of my wardrobe, see the faded jeans hanging up and thus recall the Genetics Mind Map.

CHAPTER
SIX

SPEED READING

SPEED READING

In this section we will look at Speed Reading...

We will give you a variety of techniques, not only to help you read faster, but also to help you read smarter!

Boosting understanding, finding and remembering the key points and with the help of your friends, multiplying your effectiveness many times over.

"Learning
to speed read effortlessly
and fluently has been claimed by
millions of people around the world to
be one of the most rewarding and
significant events of
their lives."

Tony Buzan
The Speed Reading Book

INFORMATION OVERLOAD

How many books do you have on your reading list?

Be honest. How many have you *ACTUALLY* read?

How do you know what's worth reading until you've read it?

Wouldn't it be great if you could read a book in an afternoon?

or even better...
Get someone else to read the books for you and tell you the important bits?

Yeah right -
Like that's really
goin' to happen!

Actually,
it will!

Do you know...

About 1,000 books are published internationally every day and the total of all printed knowledge doubles every five years.

Then there are reports, newspapers, magazines, journals, plus the massive explosion of material on the World Wide Web.

So how fast do I need to read to cope with this?

The average reading speed is between 150 words per minute and 240 words per minute.

The United Nations stated that to keep pace with all the information you would need to read at 400 wpm (but this was before the advent of e-mail, the Internet and texting)

An easy target to aim for is 1000 words per minute. However, with practice you can read at over 3000wpm

BELIEFS

Have you ever been told...

INTRODUCTION

INFORMATION
OVERLOAD

☞ BELIEFS

GUIDES

UNDERSTANDING

R&R FOR
THE RETINA

BOOK BLITZ

SUMMARY

✗ Saying the words under your breath slows you down.

✓ *Saying words under your breath can help you remember - especially if you mentally shout out important bits.*

✗ Pointing at words with your finger is childish.

✓ *As we'll see later, finger pointing dramatically increases speed.*

✗ Read "slowly and carefully".

✓ *Reading quickly can increase your understanding.*

✗ Begin at the beginning and go through to the end.

✓ *You can learn more by just picking out important stuff from a book.*

✗ Go back and reread or look up anything you don't understand before you carry on.

✓ *Interrupting your flow reduces understanding and slows you down.*

✗ Read one word at a time.

✓ *You can easily read several words at a time.*

✗ You should understand everything you read.

✓ *100% comprehension is hardly ever necessary.*

✗ You can only read what your eyes are focusing on.

✓ *You can see an entire page with a single glance and take in more than you may think.*

✗ Never write on books.

✓ *A good way to engage with a book is to highlight words and make notes in the margins.*

Anne Jones has won the Mind Sports Olympiad reading tournament six times in row.

What's more, she only uses the techniques that we'll show you!

THE EYES

A typical reader's eyes move something like this when they read as piece of text…

Jumping from word to word resting on each,

sometimes they skip backwards,

or even wander off the page completely.

The way to speed up your reading is to avoid all these bad habits. Let us explain…

GROUPS OF WORDS

If you take in groups of words at a time instead of reading the words one by one you can greatly increase your speed. Even if you only took in two at a time that would double your speed and it's possible to take in six or more!

FIXATION TIME

A fixation is the name given to the stops in-between jumps when the eye recognises each word (or group of words). These last for anything between a quarter and one and a half seconds. If you can halve the time each fixation takes you can double your speed again!

ONLY GOING FORWARDS

Every time you back skip you waste time. So make an effort to only move forwards.

STAY ON THE PAGE

This sounds obvious, but by keeping your attention on the page and not allowing your eyes and thoughts to wander, you can improve your speed still further.

On the next page we'll give you a technique to help you to do all these things…

INTRODUCTION

INFORMATION
OVERLOAD

BELIEFS

☞ GUIDES

UNDERSTANDING

R&R FOR
THE RETINA

BOOK BLITZ

SUMMARY

GUIDES

When you learned to read you probably used your finger to point to the words as you read them.

It was a good technique and worked very well until one day your teacher said something like, "Now you know how to read take your finger off the page because pointing at the words slows you down".

Surely a better thing to have done would have been to move your finger faster!

Your eyes are designed to follow moving objects. When you catch a ball, you don't see lots of static images - Your eyes follow and track it and help you move your hands into the right position (hopefully) to catch it.

Your eyes can move much more smoothly if they have something to follow. This could be your finger, a pencil or a chopstick. The benefit of a long slender guide is that it doesn't cover up what's coming next so you can see a preview of text up ahead before you actually read it.

The really great thing about using a guide is that it helps you apply the other techniques that we have just talked about:

GROUPS OF WORDS
By starting a little way in from the left and stopping a little way in from the right you are forcing your eyes to take in groups of words at the start and end of lines.

FIXATION TIME
The faster you move the guide the shorter your fixation times will be.

ONLY GOING FORWARDS
You don't have to be a genius for this one!

STAY ON THE PAGE
Keep you guide on the page and keep your eyes on your guide.

 THINGS TO AVOID
Don't "tap out" words as you read them - move your guide in a smooth flowing motion under the words.

Don't use your guide like a ruler as this stops you seeing what's coming up. Instead use it as a pointer, so your eye follows the tip.

UNDERSTANDING

INTRODUCTION

INFORMATION
OVERLOAD

BELIEFS

GUIDES

☞ UNDERSTANDING

R&R FOR
THE RETINA

BOOK BLITZ

SUMMARY

No matter how fast you read, if you don't understand any of it then there isn't any point in reading it!

One of the benefits of speeding up is that you can actually improve your understanding.

Every word or idea can be the starting point for the brain to make lots of associations. If you read too slowly then you are giving your brain plenty of time to make many associations, most of which will have nothing to do with the text. The faster you go the closer you are to understanding the author's intent and associations!

Another way to boost understanding is to reread the text. If you're reading at twice your usual speed, you can read the text twice in the same amount of time.

Try not to make rereading a habit. It not only defeats one the the reasons for speed reading - to free up more of your time - but also reduces your concentration. World Memory Champion Dominic O'Brien explains...

In my act I
memorise words called out
by the audience. In theory, the longer I
take, the clearer the image and so the
stronger the memory, but if there's too long a gap
between words it throws my concentration.
Because I know I'm only going to hear each
word once, it forces me to focus my mind
more...

Likewise, when reading, by speeding
up you get into a rhythm which aids
concentration and so increases understanding.
Tell yourself that you're only going to read each
sentence once, otherwise you're telling your
mind that it doesn't have to focus so hard
the first time.

INTRODUCTION

INFORMATION
OVERLOAD

BELIEFS

GUIDES

UNDERSTANDING

R&R FOR
THE RETINA

BOOK BLITZ

SUMMARY

RESTING THE EYES

Just like any other muscle the eyes need rest, especially when you have been reading or studying for a long while.

To refresh your eyes...

Rub your hands together briskly, until the palms are quite warm.

Lean forward on your elbows, cupping your hands over your closed eyes, resting lightly.

Think of blackness; black velvet; a black cat; deep dark night.

Rest like this for at least one minute.

Open your eyes and feel refreshed!

'Where shall I begin, please
your Majesty?' he asked. 'Begin at
the beginning,' said the King, gravely,
'and go on till you come to the end:
then stop.'

Lewis Carroll
Alice in Wonderland

This advice may have been the best available in 1865
when Lewis Carroll wrote 'Alice in Wonderland'.

We now know that the best way to get the information
from a book, especially a text book, isn't to read from
beginning to end. Instead, work from the sections, to
the chapters, to the headings in the text, to the details.

We'll show you how in the Book Blitz on the next
page…

BOOK BLITZ

With a group of friends
select a book each

Look at the cover of your book

Sections become main
branches

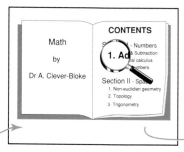

Find the chapters of the book

These become third
level branches

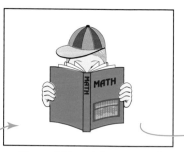

Speed Read the rest of
the text.

Decide on a central image

Find the sections of the book

Math
by
Dr A. Clever-Bloke

CONTENTS
Section I · Numbers
1. ... Subtraction
2. Differential calculus
3. Complex numbers

Section II · Space
1. Non-euclidian geometry
2. Topology
3. Trigonometry

Chapters become
second level branches

In each chapter find any
headings in the text

Polynom

Add details

Copy Mind Maps and
share with friends
(each person explain theirs)

Celebrate

INTRODUCTION

INFORMATION
OVERLOAD

BELIEFS

GUIDES

UNDERSTANDING

R&R FOR
THE RETINA

BOOK BLITZ

SUMMARY

SUMMARY

The speed reading techniques can be summarised with the acronym
GO FASTER...

Guide

Using a guide allows the eyes to move in a smoother way and helps with the other techniques.

Only Forwards

Back skipping wastes time and should be avoided. If you think you missed something keep going. It is very likely that you will understand what was meant by the context or the same point will often be repeated later.

Fixations Shorter

The less time your eyes spend resting on each word (or group of words) the faster you will read.

Allow Information to Come to You

Imagine reading as being like a sponge soaking up information rather than having to go out to grab it. This makes the process easier and much less stressful.

Stay on the Page

Keep your focus on the page. If you have problems concentrating make sure you take regular breaks and remember to rest your eyes when you start to get tired.

Take in Groups of Words

Practise increasing the number of words that you take in one go. If you can currently manage two, try three. You should eventually be able to get up to about six words at a time.

Enjoy

Everything, including reading is easier if it's fun. If you're not enjoying it, your thoughts will be elsewhere and you won't remember what you have read - So why did you waste the time reading it?

Reason for Reading

Before you start reading, decide what you want to get out of the text. Are there specific questions you need answering? Once you have a purpose, your brain will alert you to what you need - The information will "leap out" at you.

CHAPTER SEVEN

SUPER STUDY SKILLS

INTRODUCTION

In this section we will look at practical ways to apply what we know about how the brain works to successful studying.

You will see how quickly your brain can forget information and how to maintain high levels of recall through correct reviews.

This builds into an easy to follow, brain friendly review system that can be applied to all your studies.

Finally we'll show you how to draw together all the strategies in this book into a single plan for working towards exam success at any level.

INTRODUCTION

☞ **MEMORY AFTER
LEARNING**

HOW TO REVISE?

THE IDEAL
STUDY HOUR

STUDYING FOR
EXAMS

MEMORY AFTER LEARNING

"Normal" students - even those with quite good grades still 'forget' most of what they have learned within 24 hours. During that time they can lose 80-90% of the detail covered - Imagine, for every hour of study, they only remember 10 minutes worth of information.

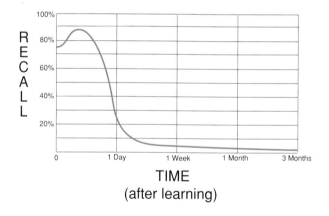

TIME
(after learning)

If you want to learn faster, work smarter and remember much more - here's how.

The easiest way to sustain your level of knowledge is to review it whilst your recall is at its peak. If you wait until your recall starts to decline then you have to relearn the information rather than merely review it.

Luckily this doesn't mean reviewing everything you have learned every day. Five reviews is enough to transfer your knowledge into long term memory. The ideal times to review are...

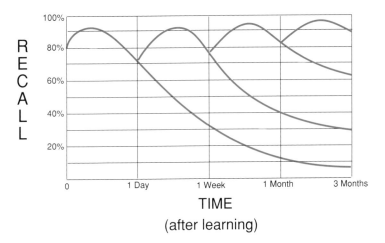

TIME
(after learning)

If you are using Mind Maps or one of the Memory Systems this entire review process can take less than 10 minutes in total. By starting to review as soon as you have learned something, you will never have to experience the panic of cramming at the last minute.

HOW TO REVISE

1 Take your notes in a memorable way (we suggest you use Mind Maps)

2 Date notes and add review codes:
   10 Minutes (10)
   Day (D)
   Week (W)
   Month (M)
   Three Months (3M)

3 Fold and punch Mind Maps for filing in your ring binder.

4 Name and number Mind Maps in sequence (eg Maths 1, Maths 2, etc)

5 File by subject

6 Write the Mind Map name and number into your diary for review tomorrow.

7 Repeat for :

   1 week's time
   1 month's time
   3 months' time

8 On completion of each review strike through the appropriate review code on the bottom of each Mind Map.

INTRODUCTION

MEMORY AFTER
LEARNING

HOW TO REVISE?

THE IDEAL
STUDY HOUR

STUDYING FOR
EXAMS

THE IDEAL
STUDY HOUR

Does it work?

Fourteen students from four South London schools approached us with a single burning ambition: "Show us what we need to get A's in our A-levels and we will do it" - and they did!

Despite three having dyslexia and one having cerebral palsy **ALL** passed their exams with flying colours - An amazing 42 'A' grades amongst them. Even more fantastic, one young lady decided to study for A-level Spanish with only six months to go before the exams "Because learning was now so easy - I wanted a new challenge"

What did they do?

Exactly what you can learn to do here.

Recall During Learning (If you take **BREAKS**)

You can boost recall by taking breaks during your learning, so the Ideal Study System must include frequent breaks.

Do some gentle physical exercise in the first break to get better blood and oxygen flow to the brain

The body is about 90% water by volume so grab a drink (ideally water) in the second break.

In the third break practise your relaxation technique to be better prepared for exams.

5   20   5   15   5   10

E X E R C I S E

D R I N K

R E L A X

0   5   25   30   45   50   60

Minutes

Spend the 20 minutes after your exercise using a study technique that works in harmony with your natural memory rhythms, ie lots of beginnings and ends, repeated and associated items and outstanding things.

Two examples of techniques that do this are Mind Mapping and the Route Memory System as both allow you to learn and recall large amounts of information easily..

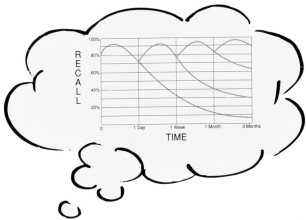

Spend the 15 minutes after your second break reviewing the Mind Maps or Routes from your files. Notes that you made yesterday, one week ago and one month ago. This won't take long, for example you can review a Mind Map in a little as 90 seconds.

"It's as important to review as to learn something new."

Linda Leckie
Student at LSE

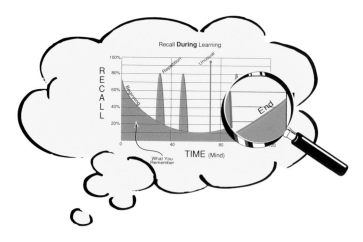

Because we recall more from the end of a session than from the middle the last 10 minutes is the ideal time for reviewing and completing the new work studied earlier. At this point you will see any gaps, additional connections or parts you do not yet understand.

EXERCISE   DRINK   REVIEW   RELAX   REVIEW

5   20   5   15   5   10

0   5   25 30   45   50   60

Minutes

REVIEW DAY WEEK MONTH

III

STUDYING FOR EXAMS

Mind Map lecture

File in folder

Redraw Mind Map

Practise routes

Eat, relax, sleep, sport, etc

Relax & good sleep night before

Review: 10 minutes
day, week, month, 3 months

Route main points

Create Mega Mind Map

Review Mega Mind Map
& routes daily

Exam

Celebrate

Further Reading

MEMORY
Use Your Memory - Tony Buzan
ISBN 0563537302

How to Pass Exams – Dominic O'Brien
ISBN 01904292399

Never Forget Facts & Figures – Dominic O'Brien
ISBN 1904292518

Never Forget A Speech – Dominic O'Brien
ISBN 190429250X

Never Forget Numbers & Dates – Dominic O'Brien
ISBN 190329682X

Learn to Remember - Dominic O'Brien
ISBN 0811827151

Essential Lifeskills: Improving Your Memory - David Thomas
ISBN 0751348953

MIND MAPPING
The Mind Map Book - Tony Buzan
ISBN 0563487011

How to Mind Map - Tony Buzan
ISBN 0007146841

Use Your Head - Tony Buzan
ISBN 056337103

Get Ahead – Vanda North with Tony Buzan
ISBN 1874374007

SPEED READING

Remember Everything You Read: The Evelyn Wood Seven-Day
Speed Reading and Learning Program - Stanley D. Frank
ISBN 0812917731

The Speed Reading Book - Tony Buzan
ISBN 056348702X

REVISION

Teach Yourself Revision Guides - various authors with Tony Buzan
Published by Hodder & Stoughton

Recommended Web Sites

COURSES AND LEARNING TO LEARN

Additional Training
www.learning-tech.co.uk
www.mindmaptraining.com
www.mind-map.com

Speed Reading
www.speedyreader.co.uk

Accelerated Learning
www.learnfast.co.uk

FINANCIAL LITERACY
www.investnshare.com

MIND SPORTS
www.worldmemorychampionship.com
www.msoworld.com

Training Services

The authors are available to run seminars in the following techniques...

Mind Mapping
Memory
Speed Reading
Creativity
Time Management
Accelerated Learning

INSET Training for Teachers
Work with groups of students
Public Open Courses

For further information call:

Phil Chambers on 07000 853276

phil@learning-tech.co.uk or visit www.learning-tech.co.uk

We also offer **Financial Literacy training** – Understanding how money works so that you can make your money work for you instead of always having to work for your money.

For further information call call:

Lawrie-Ann Blair on 01334 650 825

info@InvestnShare.com or visit www.InvestnShare.com

Also by the Authors

A Mind to do Business

The face of business is changing so rapidly that life-long learning has become essential. Our new portfolio careers bring the additional stress of having to continually update our skill-sets to keep our future employment prospects high. The necessity of juggling a full-time job and training requirements with family and home life can push some of us to breaking point.

This book gives you the necessary tools to take control of the information that bombards you on a daily basis; to manage your time; to remember, think and learn more effectively.

Presented in a highly visual and yet structured format with numerous business examples, it allows the reader to quickly grasp and begin to apply the techniques.

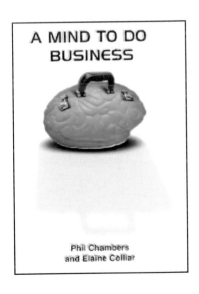

Thank **** it Wasn't Tammy Wynette - The Single Mom's Guide to Financial Freedom

The story of how Elaine went from being left at Heathrow Airport with her infant son and £70, to financial independence a mere three years later. This book will show you how she learned the skills necessary to achieve her dream. It will help you to set your own goals and learn how to achieve whatever you desire for your own life.

The Single Mom's Guide to... series of 'pocket' books:

... Designing your life

... Financial Literacy

... Creating Assets

... Property Development

... Buy-to-let Properties

... Stock Market Investing

... Options Trading

... Building a Business